The Story of
Harry
A World War Two Evacuee

Andrew Donkin

Illustrated by Linda Clark

WAYLAND

Chronology of
Harry's Battle of Britain

1939 1 September After years of building up his forces, the German leader, Adolf Hitler, invades Poland.
3 September Britain and France are forced to declare war on Germany. In Britain children are evacuated from the cities to the countryside. Ration books for food are issued. Gas masks are distributed to every man, woman and child.

September 1939 – May 1940 The period known as the 'Phoney War', so-called because both sides are preparing their forces for the real conflict that is to come.
10 May Germany invades Belgium and the Netherlands before attacking France. France falls to Germany in less than 3 weeks. Retreating British and French troops are evacuated from Dunkirk, France, on **26 May**.

Early July 1940 *The Battle of Britain* begins as the German air force, the Luftwaffe, starts its regular attacks on British airfields, radar stations, sea ports and factories. Hitler's aim is to wipe out the British air force – the only thing that is capable of stopping his invading army.

With thanks to the Imperial War Museum,
Duxford

This edition first published in Great Britain in
1999 by Macdonald Young Books, an imprint of
Wayland Publishers Limited, original title:
Harry's Battle of Britain

Re-issued in 2008 by Wayland

Reprinted in 2010 (twice) and 2011 by Wayland

Printed in China

Wayland
338 Euston Road,
London NW1 3BH

ISBN 978 0 7502 5431 1

Wayland is a division of Hachette Children's Books,
an Hachette UK Company

www.hachette.co.uk

Chapter One

Sent Away.

September 1939

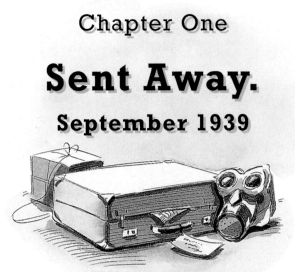

The only good thing about it was
at least we were all going together.
Our whole class was being sent away
to escape the Nazi war machine.

All over Britain, schoolchildren were
being taken to live in the countryside.
Altogether, nearly a million children
were on the move, all of them about to
become evacuees.

Britain was now at war with
Germany and everyone knew that
pretty soon the Germans would start
attacking and bombing our cities.

The bus had left the city behind and had been going down country lane after country lane for hours. It felt like we were being taken to the ends of the earth.

I was sitting next to my best friend, Bobby. He looked even more worried than me. Bobby saw me watching him and shrugged his shoulders hopelessly. There was nothing left to say. No one wanted to leave home.

My Dad had told me that the only things between us and a German invasion were the English Channel and our air force.

As we drove along, I looked out of the window and imagined dozens of Nazi paratroopers in steely-grey uniforms suddenly swarming out of the woods and surrounding our bus.

Just the thought of England being invaded and everyone being captured made me feel sick.

When we arrived at what was to be 'our' village we trooped off the bus. A man with a clipboard said he was the Billeting Officer in charge of us and began to call our names.

"Harry Adams?"

"Here, Sir," I shouted.

We were marched inside the village hall where there were tables with milk and sandwiches. I didn't realise how hungry I was until I saw them.

"Listen," said Bobby urgently as we started on the food.

Outside, I heard the bus engine starting up. As the bus drove away a murmur went around the hall. We were here to stay.

After a while people from the surrounding area began to trickle into the hall. They took a look around at us and then pointed at the children they had chosen.

"They're picking all the big kids," whispered Bobby, after an hour or so of painful waiting. I began to wonder what would happen if it got to the end and nobody had picked you.

"Maybe we should say we're brothers so we don't get split up?" I said.

Bobby gave me a scared look.

"But what if they find out we're not? Then we'll get it."

I saw with surprise that there was a man looking down at me.

"Okay, son?" he said, and I realised with a mixture of relief and horror that I had been chosen.

"I'm Mr Scott," said the man lifting me on to the back of his tractor that was waiting outside. "Hold on tight."

I looked back towards Bobby as we drove away, but the lights of the village hall were quickly swallowed by the country twilight.

Chapter Two

Ambush.

December 1939

Winter seemed to close in fast as I settled into life on the Scotts' farm. Their grown-up son was away doing training in the army somewhere and I had his room.

Mr and Mrs Scott were good to me, but it wasn't like being at home with Mum and Dad. Apart from missing them, the strangest thing was getting used to the animals. The whole day revolved around feeding, watering, milking and herding them about.

Between all the work, I still had to go to the village school for lessons. Afterwards I always met up with Bobby, just like at home.

"How's things?"
"Okay," he lied.

I knew that he was having a far worse time of it than me and that he had loads more work to do at his foster-parents' stables.

The three months we'd been away from home had crawled by, but now it was only a week until Christmas.

As we walked back from school, our shoes left sharp, clear footprints in the white frost. Mum was coming to visit on Christmas Day and I couldn't wait to see her.

"Harry, when do you think the war will end?" said Bobby suddenly.

"I dunno, Bobby. Mr Scott told me maybe Easter. "That's not long," I said... "OUCH!"

A ball of ice and grit suddenly stung the back of my neck and we heard laughter from the trees behind us.

"Ambush!" I whispered to Bobby. "Get your gun."

After school the village was the battleground for a running war between 'them' and 'us' – 'us' being the evacuees and 'them' being the country kids.

I slid my carved, wooden machine gun out of my school bag and ran towards the laughter.

There, waiting for us, was the enemy – four local boys each holding an armful of dirtballs made of ice and grit.

"You're gonna get it now," said the leader, a boy called Jack Rodgers.

He threw a dirtball straight at me and I batted it away, cricket style, with my machine gun.

In one smooth movement I raised my gun and fired off a round of a hundred pretend bullets point blank into his chest.

"Missed!" he smirked, unleashing another dirtball.

Behind us, I heard the sound of heavy footsteps running and the smiles of our enemies started to disappear.

Reinforcements at last.

"Get 'em, Bob!" I shouted.

The enemy turned and fled as the rest of our gang arrived. We caught two of them down by the drainage ditch and stuffed their own dirtballs down their backs.

Bobby had a big grin on his face as we watched them scarper.

My good mood lasted until I got back to the farm. There was a letter from Mum and I ripped it open to see when she was arriving.

But it wasn't that kind of letter. Dad had finally been called up into the army and Mum had been promoted in the ammunitions factory where she worked. They couldn't spare her over the holidays.

It felt like Christmas had just been cancelled.

Chapter Three
It Begins.
April 1940

As spring was turning to summer we saw our real enemy for the first time.

The voices on the radio said that the 'Phoney War' was now over and that the fighting was about to begin.

Every week we watched more and more warplanes buzzing across the sky like angry insects. Bobby and I became experts on the shapes of their wings and the sounds of their engines.

Usually we could identify a plane while it was still a dot on the horizon.

Usually. Until one day.

It was a Thursday and we were all out playing by the old water tower after school.

The tower had been stripped of all its metal for the war effort ages ago. Now it was abandoned and made a brilliant base for the gang.

Recently the two gangs of 'us' and 'them' had become just us. After seven long months, it seemed that everybody was closing ranks.

Bobby and I were inside the tower base, carving the barrel of a anti-aircraft gun out of a large, wooden fence post.

Jack heard them first and stood up, scanning the horizon.

"Hurricanes?" said Tom.

"No. The engine noise is too deep," dismissed Jack.

As I listened, I could hear that he was right.

Then we saw them, three black dots sweeping towards us across an otherwise blue sky.

As they drew closer we realised with a sinking feeling that they weren't Hurricanes or Spitfires, or anything we'd ever seen before.

"They're not ours, are they?" whispered Bobby.

Three German Messerschmitts flew over our heads, engines screaming.

The leading plane had a Nazi swastika on its tail, a black German cross on its body and giant teeth – like a shark's jaws – painted at its front.

"Maybe they're lost?" suggested Tom.

"Or going to attack Westholt airfield?" added Jack, instantly wishing he hadn't said it.

Westholt airfield was just over the horizon and suddenly I desperately wanted to be able to warn everyone there. But the planes would be there in just a few minutes and there was nothing that any of us could do.

It was a terrible thing. Just to know that the Nazis could come and fly over your country, over your school, even over your home whenever they felt like it.

In bed that night, I couldn't get those planes out of my mind. I lay awake for ages, staring up into the utter darkness of the blacked-out room.

Suddenly a tap on the window half scared me to death and I snatched back the blackout curtain.

"Bobby?"

He was holding a bag and I could see that he'd been crying.

"I'm running away," he said.

"Where?"

"Home. Proper home. If the Nazis can get us here, we might as well go back."

I tried to get him to change his mind but I couldn't. In the end, I gave him all the money I had, although it wasn't very much.

"I'll write to you," he said, and his small figure slipped away into the utter dark of night in the countryside.

It took me 'til dawn to get to sleep.

Chapter Four

Attack.

July 1940

School was over for the summer and after we'd done our chores – helping with the milking in my case – the gang would meet at the water tower.

We had turned it into a real base, with all sorts of old junk and stuff.

Wooden anti-aircraft guns poked through the four main gun ports, ready for action. When we spotted an enemy plane, two of us would swing the gun around and follow its path through the sky while someone else gave the order to "Fire!"

By July, we saw battles in the sky nearly every day. Green and brown Spitfires would duck and weave through the squadrons of enemy aircraft that outnumbered and outgunned them.

We kept count as closely as we could. In spite of the difference in numbers, the Spitfires were shooting down two, or even three enemy planes for every one of them that was lost.

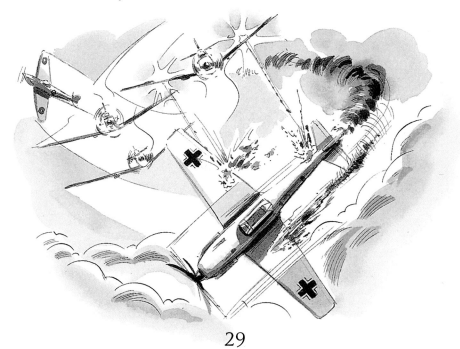

There was no news of Bobby. He didn't write. Eventually, the other kids had stopped asking me about him because they could see that I didn't want reminding all the time.

One afternoon, Jack and I were carrying an old school chair back to the water tower when we heard the now-familiar buzz of enemy aircraft coming over the horizon.

"They're early today," said Jack, casually.

As we dropped the chair and began to run back to base, a wave of Junkers, German dive-bombers, howled over our heads. Then another wave appeared behind them, followed by another and then by still more.

We'd never seen so many in the air at once.

"Must be half the Luftwaffe," I said, watching them go over.

31

By the time we got back to the
tower, the summer sky was black with
squadrons of enemy bombers, all
guarded by smaller fighter planes.

Hitler had obviously decided to start
the real war.

"Look!" shouted Jack, his voice full
of excitement and hope, "Spitfires."

The battle was now being joined by British fighter planes. The pilots were careful to position themselves between the bright sun and the German aircraft so they could use the sun as cover.

The Spitfires, which were more manoeuvrable and faster, took on the German fighter planes, while the Hurricanes attacked the bombers. The whole sky above us crackled with one-on-one dogfights.

"Come on, let's man the guns,"
said Jack.

We tried to shoot at just about every
German aircraft in the sky. In my mind,
I saw the enemy plummet to earth in a
burst of flame and smoke.

A grey Messerschmitt passed low over our base, chasing a Spitfire with one of its engines on fire.

We followed the Messerschmitt's path with our guns. It banked into a steep turn and angled around.

Then the roar of its engines changed tone and I knew with absolute certainty and terror what was about to happen.

The pilot had seen our base and our wooden guns and thought they were the real thing. The plane had turned to face us and I realised he was beginning his run to attack our water tower.

Chapter Five

Real War.
Real Bullets.
REAL CLOSE.

"Push them out!" I shouted.

"What?"

"Push the guns out – so the pilot'll see they're not real. Quick!"

But it was too late.

The aircraft was coming in low and fast. A spray of machine-gun bullets smashed a path of destruction through the field, heading straight towards us.

"Get down!"

We threw ourselves on to the floor as the machine-gun fire ripped into the tower all around us. It felt as if the whole tower was exploding from the inside out.

I couldn't tell where the deafening roar of the bullets ended and the pounding of my heart began.

My ears were ringing and I could hardly hear myself as I shouted, "Is everyone okay?"

Somehow no one had been hit. This time.

Through one of the gun windows we saw the Messerschmitt begin to turn for a second run.

We froze to the spot.
  Then as it banked, its
tail and left wing were
suddenly and completely
shot to pieces.

A cloud of thick, black smoke erupted from the plane's under-carriage and it went into a short tailspin before crashing into the distant green of Crossly Woods.

I felt the explosion rumble up through my knees and up into the pit of my stomach.

No one spoke as we watched the thickening column of smoke rise above the trees.

Finally Jack said simply, "Better get home then."

We left the water tower without another word. I took my time walking home. I was in a bit of a daze.

The air battle had moved north over the horizon. I couldn't see it anymore, but I could still hear some of the explosions.

"About time, young Harry," said Mr Scott when I got back to the farm. "There's something inside for you," he announced, like he had a surprise Christmas present to give me.

In the farmhouse there was the smell of freshly baked bread in the air as always – and there was something else.

"Mum!"

Mum was sitting at the kitchen table talking to Mrs Scott.

"I brought someone with me," she said casually and pointed at the back door.

"Hello Harry," said a small voice rather sheepishly.

It was Bobby.

"Your mum brought me back. Looks like you're going to have to share your room," he grinned.

They'd been talking to the Billeting Officer and Mr and Mrs Scott were going to let Bobby stay with me on the farm.

As I hugged Mum, a deep booming engine noise flew low over the farmhouse. I knew it was the German aircraft returning home battered and bruised from the fighting.

We weren't going to be invaded. At least not today. Still, I hugged Mum extra tight anyway, just to make sure.

Further Information

The Battle of Britain is the name given to the World War 2 air battle between German and British air forces over Britain. The battle lasted from early July until 31 October 1940. The Germans had the advantage because they had seized airfields in the Netherlands, Belgium and France, which were safe from attack and from which they could easily attack south-east England.

On 1 August the Luftwaffe (German air force) had about 4,500 aircraft, compared to about 3,000 planes for the Royal Air Force (RAF). The main battle was fought between the RAF's fighters – Hurricanes and Spitfires – and the Luftwaffe's Messerschmitt 109s and bombers – Dornier 17s, Heinkel 111s, and Junker 88s. Between August-September 1940 the total number of planes lost were:

for the RAF   832 fighters
for the Luftwaffe   1733 planes

Hitler's aim was for the Luftwaffe to destroy the British air force before the German invasion. His plan was thwarted by the particular success of British fighters in shooting down his bombers. The German fighter planes did not carry enough fuel for long flying missions and so were not able to protect their bombers. The loss of so many bombers meant that in October 1940 Hitler was forced to abandon his plan for an invasion of Britain. He chose instead to invade the USSR (Russia). Recognising the bravery of the Battle of Britain pilots, Prime Minister Winston Churchill said, "Never in the field of human conflict was so much owed by so many to so few."